SHAQ

SHAQ

PETER C. BJARKMAN

SMITHMARK

This edition published in 1994
by SMITHMARK Publishers Inc.,
16 East 32nd Street,
New York, New York 10016

SMITHMARK books are available for bulk purchase for sales promotion and premium use. For details write or telephone the Manager of Special Sales, SMITHMARK Publishers Inc., 16 East 32nd Street, New York, NY 10016. (212) 532-6600.

Produced by Brompton Books Corp.,
15 Sherwood Place,
Greenwich, CT 06830

ISBN 0-8317-7983-7

Printed in China

10 9 8 7 6 5 4 3 2 1

For my daughter, Kimberly Dale Bjarkman, who finds her own pop culture heroes in a different arena

Previous pages: Shaquille O'Neal displays both the awesome power (page 1) *and towering stature* (page 2) *that have made him the NBA's newest sensation.*

These pages: Shaq muscles for position under the boards (page 4) *in game action with the Charlotte Hornets. Later in the same contest* (page 5) *he rejects a power shot by the Hornets' Larry Johnson.*

CONTENTS

INTRODUCTION

Almost overnight he has become America' most popular athlete of the mid-1990s, and it is a measure of his unprecedented success that he is known everywhere by but a single name – Shaq.

In only two seasons, 22-year-old Shaquille O'Neal of the Orlando Magic has taken the NBA by storm. He has achieved instantaneous stardom like no other slam dunking or hot shooting basketballer ever has

before. Just as Magic Johnson and Larry Bird arrived to save a struggling pro basketball league little more than a full decade ago, so has Shaq O'Neal – with the suddenness of one of his explosive and rim-shattering dunks – taken America's most popular present-day sport to dizzying new heights.

In the process of emerging as the NBA's new show-case centerpiece Shaq has also become far more than

Left: *Shaq descends with full vengeance after one of his thundering rookie dunks versus the Hawks in Atlanta's Omni Arena.*

Right: *Few defenders can handle Shaq's power moves in close to the hoop, a fact that Atlanta forward John Koncak is about to discover.*

Left: *Dapper Shaq the rap artist poses with model Cindy Crawford after the two jointly presented a plaque for Best Dance Video at the 1993 MTV Video Music Awards.*

Top right: *Shaq shares a laugh with Bulls superstar Michael Jordan in February 1993. With Jordan's retirement at the end of the season, Shaq became the undisputed king of pro basketball.*

Right: *Shaq mixes with young fans at a Baton Rouge day care center on his own 18th birthday. Shaq posed with these children shortly after one national magazine called the LSU star "nothing more than a big kid."*

a mere basketball star. The 7-foot, 300-pound young-ster with the infectious grin has also become the nation's most widely recognized new media celebrity. O'Neal is a successful rap artist and a budding movie star to boot, as well as a fixture in dozens of popular television and print-media commercials for all man-ner of products. Teenage fans across the country hip-hop to the sounds of his rap CD, *Shaq Diesel*, and lined up outside theaters everywhere to catch the first showings of the 1994 film *Blue Chips*, in which Shaq portrays a thinly disguised version of himself. In such a short time, O'Neal has already met and largely sur-passed the immense on-court and off-court popular-ity enjoyed by Michael "Air" Jordan throughout the late 1980s and early 1990s.

Only a few star athletes have ever enjoyed such wide celebrity that they have been universally recognized throughout the world by a single colorful nickname. Baseball, of course, had its "Babe" (Ruth) during its Golden Age of the Roaring '20s. Football celebrated "Juice" (O. J. Simpson) throughout much of its own heyday in the 1970s. And basketball was dominated by the irrepressible personality of "Magic" (Johnson) across much of the 1980s — at the very hour when the NBA first surged to its present-day level of national prominence.

The 1990s, in turn, already belong to the towering muscular figure of the Shaq. He is the first athlete to trademark his seemingly endless endorsed merchan-dise under his popular and unique nickname. A skill-ful management team employed by O'Neal has de-signed a distinctive SHAQ-ATTAQ logo which now adorns pairs of Reebok basketball shoes and dozens of other products he endorses. In this last decade of the 20th century America's athletes — especially its basketball players — have become the largest marquee names in a celebrity-oriented era. And certainly no such athlete is a bigger marketing and promotional success — as well as a larger hero to American youth — than basketball's Shaquille O'Neal.

Shaq literally burst on the NBA scene in the summer and fall of 1992 as professional basketball's newest and hottest megastar. No newcomer has ever become quite such an instant success in a sport long built around individual headline performers. Certainly no first-timer was ever so widely conceded to be the league's "rookie sensation" even before the opening center jump of the new season.

And the newest NBA headliner immediately lived up to his advance billing. In the first month of the season he had already established his unstoppable dominance over other outsized and overmatched pivotmen. As a green rookie he was a landslide All-Star Game selection, helped out of course by immense media coverage of his early-season on- and off-court exploits. And by year's end his impressive numbers

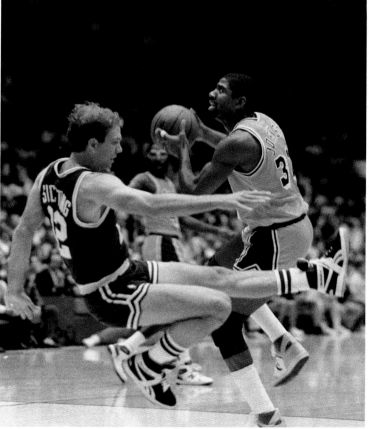

more than justified every bit of the enthusiastic pre-season and early-season hype.

Other NBA stars of the past have also enjoyed fabulous freshman campaigns. Bill Russell in the space of several months established a new respecta-bility for defense and overhauled the fortunes of a lackluster Boston Celtics franchise. Oscar Robertson and Jerry West later burned up the league with their scoring onslaughts as newcomers on the block. But these three great stars of the early 1960s had all per-formed in relative obscurity, playing a sport that was still relatively "minor league" in national status.

Magic and Bird also immediately took over the NBA scene in their debut seasons. But their celebrity status had grown over several seasons and was not in-stantaneous. Magic and Bird first had to replace initial novelty with lasting adulation by leading their clubs in Los Angeles and Boston to coveted league championships. Thus they earned their first lasting hold on greatness in league post-season play. Shaq — admittedly aided by the new prominence which Bird and Magic brought to the sport of pro basketball — was a phenomenon from the very moment his "official" career was launched with 1992's NBA Draft Day.

Michael Jordan had also entered the league with something of a loud bang. And yet it admittedly took Jordan several seasons to earn his wings of flight and truly establish his high-scoring game before disbe-

Left: *Shaq has constantly been compared from the first to the game's big-man legends of the past. Boston Celtics star Bill Russell (top left) was once the kind of intimidator Shaq was now expected to become. And Michael Jordan (left) and Earvin "Magic" Johnson (bottom left) had established the role of basketball star as media celebrity which Shaq was now destined to fill.*

Below: *Already a seasoned world traveler as well as a nation's sports idol, Shaq poses in front of Big Ben in London in October 1993. Shaq's Orlando Magic team was in England to take on the Atlanta Hawks in a set of exhibition games as the NBA began taking its new bigger-than-life headliner on the road.*

lieving NBA fans. Jordan, after all, played for a brief while in the shadow of Larry Bird and Magic Johnson. No one anticipated how great Michael might eventually be when he first debuted his incredible airborne style of play for the lowly Chicago Bulls. But the retirement of all three — Magic, Bird and now Michael — had suddenly left the field wide open for Shaq at the end of his superb rookie-year performance. Unexpectedly the league was again in need of an attractive superstar to carry its banner. And NBA marketing gurus had already found and fostered just such a showcase star in the huge center now playing for the Orlando Magic expansion franchise.

Shaq, by contrast with Jordan, has already taken over America's new "favorite sport" — a status he already enjoyed even as a twenty-year-old untried rookie. What he has achieved so far on the NBA court has been nothing short of awesome and altogether unparalleled in the annals of sport history. His off-court celebrity is also unprecedented for a newcomer in any sport. Shaquille O'Neal is undoubtedly America's biggest sports star of the 1990s. Even at the end of but two full NBA seasons his blinding star was already fixed firmly in the basketball firmament, and his story has just begun to unfold.

PART I
SHAQ-NIFICENT—THE BIRTH OF A BASKETBALL SENSATION

The transition from college stardom to professional status is often traumatic for the young athlete. Many a collegiate superstar has failed outright and disappeared from the limelight overnight. Others have found the whirlwind lifestyle and temptations of money and a fast-paced social life ruinous to top-level performance on the court or in the stadium. Most have quickly exchanged the mantle of a superstar for that of just another everyday player.

This falling off of performance level and attending glory is often especially dramatic if the athlete has left college early and suddenly finds himself a major media celebrity at barely twenty years of age, as Shaquille O'Neal did. There is the rigor of life on the road to contend with. There is the constant nuisance and temptation of hangers-on who surround the rising superstar and all want some small piece of the action. And there is the added pressure of standing alone in a much more demanding national forum which is as quick to condemn and chastise as it is to praise and celebrate. The national audience is always much more skeptical and cynical than is the blindly loyal flock of hometown campus rooters.

For Shaquille O'Neal, however, this transition was

Right: *The latest NBA rookie sensation, Shaquille O'Neal, receives a red carpet introduction on All-Star Saturday in 1993. While Shaq's first All-Star appearance would not be a smashing on-court success, he was still the off-court hit of a gala weekend in Utah.*

Left: *O'Neal scores over Chicago Bulls defenders Scottie Pippen (33) and Bill Cartwright (24) at legendary Chicago Stadium.*

perhaps not quite so abrupt as it often is for others. Shaq had practically lived on the road from his earliest childhood years. And as a youngster who towered above the crowd at 6'6" before his 13th birthday, he always attracted attention from the earliest years of his nomadic life.

Shaq was born in the least glamorous of places — the run-down and dangerous inner-city projects of Newark, New Jersey. The challenges of his earliest years were underscored by family events as well as by undesirable geography. His parents had not yet married but were planning their wedding when the young father, who had recently signed up for military service, was unexpectedly shipped overseas. Thus before he could marry his schoolgirl sweetheart and take full responsibility for his child, Philip Harrison had to leave both behind and report reluctantly for his most inconvenient army assignment. Shaq's unwed mother thus provided her son's family name of O'Neal. And it was Lucille O'Neal who also searched through books to select a distinctive first name for her first-born son. The choice she made seems a fortuitous one in hindsight, for Shaquille Rashaun is an Arabic name meaning "Little Warrior."

The aptly named youngster would not be left in a fatherless home in the Newark projects for very long. Philip Harrison returned to marry Lucille O'Neal and to adopt his son as soon as an army furlough allowed. Before long the young army drill sergeant was taking his new family on the road to Germany to join him in his military assignment and share his nomadic military life style.

Shaq experienced a most unconventional childhood at his army-base homes spread around the German countryside. For one thing, his already overwhelming size as a pre-teenager meant constant taunting from classmates and strangers, especially when most of the local youngsters viewed him as a foreign intruder from America. He would also face frequent displays of anti-American sentiment at a very early age. But two positive factors arose out of these early years in Germany. The first and easily the most important was the constant and shaping discipline provided by his stern but loving father. As a 6'5" 250-pound drillmaster Sergeant Harrison was as formidable a presence with his children as with his troops. The second was a chance meeting with Louisiana State University basketball coach Dale Brown, who happened to be visiting the base near Fulda to stage a goodwill-tour basketball clinic. It was there that the LSU mentor received the shock of his life. Asking for the rank of a boyish-looking recruit who towered over him at the clinic, Coach Brown received a most stunning response. "I don't have a rank, sir, I'm only thirteen years old."

A few years later, when Shaquille reappeared as a budding star high school player in San Antonio, Texas, Brown would quickly renew his interest in the talented youngster he had once met by chance in Germany. Brown and his assistant, Craig Carse, hastily renewed their contracts as O'Neal's schoolboy fame began to spread. Coach Brown had been impressed enough during his German visit to discuss the solid academic offerings on the Louisiana campus with

Shaq's interested father. Sergeant Harrison, for his part, knew precisely what he wanted out of a first-rate college education for his son. With this combination there was little question from early on that Shaq would eventually play his college basketball on the campus of Louisiana State University.

Coach Brown was hardly the only one to take notice of O'Neal's brief but brilliant high school athletic career. Shaq arrived at Robert Cole High School at Fort Sam Houston just in time for his junior year of studies and of basketball eligibility. A military-base school near San Antonio, Cole had received a steady flow of top athletes. But there is constant instability at such an institution as talented youngsters come

and go almost overnight, following a father's shifting military assignments. At first the wary coaching staff headed by Dave Madura was not about to get too excited about another in a long line of potential prospects. But with the arrival of the huge junior from Germany, Coach Madura and his staff instantly knew they had the makings of a most special team.

Cole High School was almost unbeatable once they took the floor for the 1987-88 season with their new centerpiece recruit. Cole and O'Neal swept by a full schedule of teams that would try almost every tactic imaginable against the new Goliath of Texas high school basketball. In the end, however, Cole would lose the final and most important game of the season.

Left: *Chosen to represent LSU athletics at a 1991 presidential rally, Shaq greets George Bush at the Pete Maravich Assembly Center. LSU coach Dale Brown is seen between Shaq and Bush.*

Right: *At only 16 years old, Shaquille O'Neal already towers above the competition. Here he takes a jump shot for Robert Cole High School in San Antonio, Texas, in 1988.*

15

In the Texas regional championships against out-manned Liberty Hill High, Shaq and his teammates stumbled in a game that would end a state championship dream. It would be a game that taught young Shaq O'Neal a most valuable and lasting lesson. Shaq had offered with youthful confidence before the contest that he might score fifty. But over-enthusiasm caused four fouls in the game's early minutes. Then Shaq missed two crucial free throws that might have still spelled victory at game's end. The embarrassed youngster had learned a painful lesson.

It was a lesson that apparently never needed repeating. Everyone on the Texas basketball scene knew that a final year for Shaq at Cole High would be nothing short of sensational. Once the campaign started the rival schools would triple-team O'Neal and again attempt every strategy to thwart his offense. As the rugged bumping and hacking defensives continued, Shaq became increasingly aggressive himself, and thus increasingly dominant. He also developed needed all-around skills, learning to pass off to unguarded teammates who could pile up dozens of uncontested baskets against defensive alignments focused on Shaq alone. The result was predictable. Cole swept through the 36-game campaign undefeated. This time around, there would be no tournament upsets. Shaq, averaging well over 30 points and 20 rebounds a contest, and his teammates cruised unchallenged to an easy state championship victory.

Left: *Coach Dave Madura watches a tense moment in a 1989 game between Cole High and Rohawks High at Randolph Air Force Base in Texas.*

Above: *Robert Cole High had a dominant defender in young Shaq O'Neal, here rejecting a Hearn High shot in March 1989 action.*

Right: *Even as a raw high schooler Shaquille was already a media magnet. Here O'Neal basks in the glow of victory after leading Cole High to a Texas State Championship in 1989.*

16

Right: *A happy O'Neal and the entire Cole High team enjoys its Texas 3-A State Championship victory over Clarksville High School.*

Below: *Shaq has just signed on with basketball coach Dale Brown and Louisiana State University in November 1988, while still a Cole High senior. In the background are his father and mother. Philip and Lucille Harrison, and (left to right) sisters Latelfah and Ayesha and brother Jamal.*

Right: *Shaq receives some "crunch-time" last-minute instructions from LSU coach Dale Brown, who considered Shaq one of his most "coachable" players ever.*

It was obvious from the outset that Shaq's career at LSU would be simply nothing short of sensational. In fact, expectations couldn't possibly have been higher around the campus of the Southeastern Conference powerhouse program that already boasted two of the nation's top collegiate players at the time of Shaq's recruitment. In sophomore guard Chris Jackson Coach Brown already boasted the country's most explosive scoring machine. In 7-footer Stanley Roberts he also had a potential game breaker who had himself been one of the nation's top five high school recruits. The tandem of Jackson, Roberts and now Shaq seemed to spell an almost automatic national championship. Few could have guessed how quickly such dreams could turn to ashes for overly optimistic LSU Tiger fans.

The problems that soon beset LSU's doomed wonder team were never ones of chemistry between Jackson, Roberts and O'Neal. During the one season the three spent together, Brown's squad served plenty of notice that it was charting a direct course toward the apex of NCAA basketball. The 1989-90 Tigers were 22-7, 12-6 in the rugged SEC, and were eventually tumbled from their Final Four crash course by a tough 94-91 second-round tournament loss to Georgia Tech. But Chris Jackson chose to depart at the end of his sophomore campaign for the lure of NBA dollars. At the same time Roberts became an academic casualty, thus leaving Shaq to carry the entire burden alone.

Judging solely by personal stats, Shaq's final two collegiate seasons can be measured as true block-

Left: *Shaq authors a classic power slam during an SEC battle with Arkansas in the Maravich Assembly Center.*

Right: *With 7-footers Shaquille O'Neal (left) and Stanley Roberts (right) both supporting diminutive shooting sensation Chris Jackson, big things were expected from Dale Brown's LSU Tigers in 1989-90. But neither Roberts (an academic casualty) nor Jackson (gone to the NBA) would be around to help Shaq and Brown for very long.*

Right: *O'Neal was already a "man among boys" at LSU, where his unstoppable inside power moves earned a 27.6 ppg average and a handful of college "Player of the Year" awards during his productive sophomore season.*

Left: *Backboard-rattling slams like this one before an ESPN national TV audience quickly turned the LSU sophomore center into a household name in 1991.*

busters. His individual scoring output more than doubled to 27.6 as a second-year-player and remained level at 24.1 for his junior campaign. This phenom whose nickname was still spelled as "Shack" when he first arrived on campus also became the first player in SEC history to lead the conference in scoring, rebounding, field-goal percentage and blocked shots all in a single season. But it was only in that high-scoring sophomore campaign that the Tigers could capture an SEC team crown, and Dale Brown's outfit never won more than 23 games in any season while Shaq was on the floor.

The problem was that once he became the whole show Shaq also became too much of a marked man. Defenses were stacked against him and he was hounded, battered and bruised by play that bordered on unsportsmanlike. In the end it wasn't much fun being the target of such nightly gang assaults, and by the end of his frustrating junior campaign Shaquille O'Neal had decided to turn professional. There was little hope of a national title without more of a supporting cast to relieve the pressure of his nightly muggings. And he had already achieved all the highest honors of the collegiate game — two-time consensus All-America; UPI, AP and *Sports Illustrated* Player of the Year; World Amateur Athlete of the Year.

For Shaq himself the decision to turn pro before his academic eligibility had expired was never a matter of money. "I was taught at a young age that if you're not having fun at something, then it's time to go." But

little did Shaq know at the time just how much fun lay immediately around the corner in the months following the upcoming NBA draft.

Michael Jordan had sneaked up on unsuspecting basketball fans when he dazzled his way through his 1984 rookie season. Shaq was already a full-scale celebrity when he entered the NBA in November 1993. Yet the question remained whether he was really quite as good as all those press clippings. Shaq, of course, was confident he had an immediate answer.

In his first week on the NBA circuit Shaquille O'Neal literally took the pro basketball circuit by storm. Though his very first game was admittedly nothing to grab the sports page headlines, his second outing was a bit more spectacular, and his third outing was nothing short of a rave sensation.

Opening night for Shaq was indeed a bit of a slow start. Facing off against the Miami Heat, the raw rookie experienced early foul trouble, played only 32 minutes, and fouled out in the fourth quarter of a tight 110-100 Magic victory. He hit but four buckets and four free throws for a mere dozen points, yet his 18 rebound caroms did earn distinction as the highest opening night total for a rookie since Bill Walton's 24 in 1974. The season's second game saw Shaq take it directly at the Washington Bullets, scoring 22 points and sweeping 15 boards while pacing a 103-98 triumph.

By his third and fourth games Shaq had already served notice that he had indeed arrived. In a losing effort against the Charlotte Hornets O'Neal erupted for 35 points by canning 15 of 25 shots. Two nights later he posted his finest overall performance of the season by registering 31 points, 21 rebounds, and four blocks in a second straight shellacking of Washington.

After his first three games Shaq already owned his first piece of NBA history. He had become the first rookie in league history to be named "Player of the Week" during his very first week on the job. Shaq's ex-

Left: *The words that LSU fans dreaded and NBA fans cheered were uttered at this April 1992 news conference. Shaq announced that he was leaving college to take his valuable act into the high-profile NBA arenas.*

Right: *Shaq powers to the basket over Philadelphia defender Andrew Lang on November 18, 1992. In O'Neal's second full week in the NBA he had already registered two eye-opening 30-point games.*

plosive start carried on throughout much of the first two months of the 1992-93 campaign. Like any untried rookie he had his down games, such as the frustrating first half of his initial Madison Square Garden encounter with Patrick Ewing. But he also had his monster moments, like the three straight 29-point games he registered during the season's second week.

Thus after only a fortnight there was substantial proof that the much-hyped "new kid on the block" was far from a mere over-blown product of public relations hype. Shaq made it clear he had arrived to play at the highest level and to give no quarter to the league's established big boys.

Of course it was equally obvious from the beginning that it would not be easy for Shaq to dominate for the remainder of a lengthy NBA season. For one thing, he was not surrounded by much of a supporting cast. It would therefore not be reasonable to expect that Shaq could singlehandedly effect the same kind of 35-game turnaround David Robinson had brought to the San Antonio Spurs in a single rookie season.

The best players the Magic had were point guard Scott Skiles and small forward Nick Anderson. Skiles was the league's 1991 "Comeback Player of the Year" and set a single-game NBA assists mark that same season; Anderson scored 30-points-plus 14 times in 1992 and was capable of an occasional 40-point outburst. But Skiles was not John Stockton or Mark Price, and Anderson had his single-digit games almost as frequently as his double-digit onslaughts. There was also three-point specialist Dennis Scott, who would soon become Shaq's closest off-court friend. But Dennis Scott was to be injured much of Shaq's rookie season and thus contributed little to Orlando's revival season.

While he was taking immediate possession of the hardwood courts with his first trip around the NBA, Shaq was also demanding a wider audience — even among Americans with little taste for the sport of basketball. Few who saw his TV ads for Pepsi and Reebok could resist the made-for-television smile and larger-than-life charm. This is an age, after all, that

Left: *An irresistible force meets an unmoveable object as Shaq defends against New York Knicks superstar Patrick Ewing in Madison Square Garden. This matchup already had fans remembering the battles between Bill Russell and Wilt Chamberlain 30 years earlier.*

Right: *Such towering defenders as Indiana's 7-footer Rik Smits (right) and Dale Davis (32) are helpless against one of Shaq's patented net-stuffers.*

demands of its heroes a rare mixture of ruthless domination and personal charm. Here indeed was what his agent, Leonard Armato, would soon call "the perfect combination of Bambi and The Terminator."

On court he would be recognized as the closest thing in three decades to a bulky resurrection of the young and awesome Wilt Chamberlain. No one was nastier with a ball in his palm and the basket just five feet away – nor had anyone ever been so ruthless as a shot-swatting defender since the titanic days of Chamberlain and Bill Russell. In front of the TV camera or in any public forum, however, he was a truly patient gentle giant, with all the charisma of Magic Johnson and Air Jordan rolled into one – and a self-effacing sense of humor to boot.

Part of Shaq's immediate irresistible charm was his playful smile and generous ways with fans of all ages. Another part was his colorful and refreshing language. He almost seemed to be some flesh-and-blood cartoon character stepping right out of the latest Walt Disney fantasy. No athlete – not even Babe Ruth in a far different and more tolerant era – has ever been more purely "Hollywood" in his style and his appearance. Shaq wooed his audience with his colorful phrases and images. Everything was either "Shaq-rific" or "Shaq-nificent" or Shaq-something. When he opened his pocketbook and brought hundreds of dinners for the homeless in Orlando, he did so on "Shaqs-giving" Day. On another occasion he mugged for the cameras by handing wigs to his teammates and dubbing the makeshift ensemble the "Shaq-son Five."

Below left: *After the Magic assured their front line success for years with the drafting of Shaq in 1992, they secured their backcourt future at the 1993 draft with Anfernee "Penny" Hardaway. The rookie from Memphis State demonstrated in 1994 that he has all the tools to become the biggest backcourt sensation since Michael Jordan.*

Right: *Long-range bomber Dennis Scott is not only one of Shaq's biggest on-court supporters along the Orlando Magic front line, but he is also Shaq's best friend away from the hardwood action.*

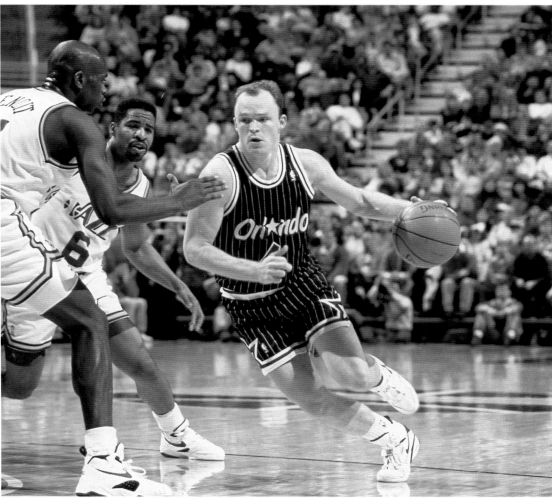

Right: *Scott Skiles would relinquish the starting point guard duties to Penny Hardaway in 1993-94, but it was Skiles who continued to supply much-needed floor and clubhouse veteran leadership for the young Orlando team.*

Shaq's heady first month of success in the NBA stretched into an anticipated eventful rookie campaign. Not only did Shaquille match and even outstretch all pre-season expectations, but his presence seemed to be reviving the previously lackluster Orlando Magic expansion team as well. By the first half of the 1992-93 NBA season Orlando was finally on the basketball map. A team that had floundered to a 10-31 All-Star break ledger a year earlier was now 21-20 at mid-course and surprisingly in the thick of the playoff race.

As the first half of the season wound down Shaq found himself locked in a heated ballot-box race with established center Pat Ewing for a starting All-Star Game berth. No rookie had cracked the starting lineup for the February classic since Jordan a decade earlier. In the end Shaq was a runaway winner by nearly a quarter million votes in the fan's poll. His first-half-season numbers seemed to merit election, no matter how much Ewing's supporters whined that Patrick's overall career stature should earn him the nod. Shaq was averaging nearly 24 points a game and rebounding at better than 14 boards per contest. He was Ewing's equal in every offense category and unquestionably of far greater value to his otherwise under-staffed team. This didn't stop Knicks coach Pat Riley from trumpeting the case for his own center by calling the rookie's selection "absurd" and "ridiculous." But it was all academic once the fans had so decisively spoken.

Left: *Shaq's charm has endeared him to fans of all ages. In this 1990 photo, Shaq enjoys an off-court moment with a group of fifth graders at the University School on the campus of LSU.*

Right: *Even Utah's rugged Karl Malone offers little resistance here as Shaq soars over "The Mailman" for another convincing bucket.*

As if to celebrate this vote of fan confidence, Shaq put on his most spectacular power performance only a few nights after All-Star rosters were announced. Playing in Phoenix against the powerhouse Suns and Charles Barkley, O'Neal accidentally pulled off an unorthodox feat that would inspire the imagination of a whole new generation of young NBA rooters. Less than a full minute into the nationally televised game Shaq got the ball and exploded over the rim for his typical bone-jarring slam — only this time he held onto the rim a moment too long and the stanchion supporting the backboard gave way. No one was more surprised than O'Neal himself when the entire backboard setup came crashing to the floor.

The centerpiece of Shaq's legendary rookie campaign would of course be an opportunity to take his "Shaq-Attaq" show on the road to the NBA All-Star Game in Utah. If no rookie had been there since Jordan, it was also apparent that no rookie had ever brought such a complete entertainment package to the league's showcase weekend. And Shaq's very first All-Star game spectacle was guaranteed to be a more glitzy venture than even Jordan's had been.

Shaquille would make the most of his All-Star headlines during festivities propping up the main event itself. At a Saturday NBA Stay in School Jam the hoops-hero-turned-rap-artist thrilled young fans in the TV audience by performing on-stage with his favorite rap group Fu Schickens. Droves of media ignored established stars while trailing the rookie everywhere in hotel lobbies and during pre-game practice. In the headline event itself Shaq was far less a factor, scoring only 13 points and playing barely 25 minutes. The always diplomatic O'Neal refused to blame limited court time on East coach Pat Riley, however. His only comment: "Shaq will be back."

Early season 1992-93 for Shaq had been crammed with headline-grabbing individual exploits. His memorable backboard-trashing event which had delayed a game for 47 minutes in Phoenix was only the first of two such displays. A second collapsed stanchion in New Jersey later in the season only added to the growing legend of the NBA's most powerful offensive force.

There was also a record-breaking single-game rebounding performance later in the season against the Washington Bullets, when Shaq rewrote the club record book with 15 first-half caroms and 25 total boards. But perhaps Shaq's finest early season moment came in Chicago during a memorable head-

to-head matchup with the game's biggest star, Michael Jordan. It was a contest in which Jordan would showcase once again why he was still the game's unchallenged superstar. Jordan wore out the nets that night with an unstoppable 64-point performance. But in the end it was also a game in which Shaq O'Neal would gain his own huge measure of newly found respect.

A week earlier Shaq had met the Bulls and Jordan for the first time before a sellout crowd on the home court in Orlando and had not fared very well at all. For the rematch in Chicago Stadium Shaq was determined to put on a more respectable show of his own. What transpired was memorable indeed. While Jordan enjoyed yet another in an endless string of stratospheric scoring performances, Shaq and the Orlando Magic fought to a thrilling overtime victory. The rookie and the expansion team proved on this particular night that they were very much for real. Shaq, not Jordan, had in the end controlled the

lengthy game with 29 points and 24 rebounds and an intimidating presence that blanketed the court from end to end. And at the end of the marathon the awesome youngster who had played more than 50 minutes didn't even appear to be the least bit tired from his herculean efforts.

The second half of the season saw the focus shift to a serious playoff run by the newly resurgent Orlando Magic. There was worry that Shaq — like so many NBA rookies unaccustomed to the lengthy pro season — would soon "hit the wall" when the season stretched out to 50, 60 or 70 games. His numbers, admittedly, did fall off some. His scoring average dipped from 24.0 to 22.1; his rebounds fell from 14.1 to 12.4; his blocked shots were cut in half and his shooting percentage dipped slightly. But Shaq insisted that he was not worn out. And some spectacular single game performances down the final stretch — like 31 points and 18 caroms against Atlanta on the season's final night — did seem to prove the point.

Left: *Basketball's immediate past and immediate future meet in mid-air as Shaq and "Air" Jordan battle above the rim in Chicago Stadium. Jordan would capture the individual battle this night with 64 points, yet Shaq and the Magic would hold their own against the World Champion Bulls with a thrilling overtime victory.*

Right: *Basketball's "tower of power" is surrounded by helpless Charlotte Hornet defenders and held only momentarily at bay.*

In the end the team fell a single game short of its goal. Shaq himself had some truly disappointing games during the team's final futile run at the last playoff position. But in the final accounting it had by almost any measure been a "magical" season for Orlando and its rookie superstar. The team had improved an even twenty games in the standings and light years in public image. The future for Magic fans now seemed limitless.

By the conclusion of his magnificent rookie year everyone – even the severest doubters – knew about the "Shaq-Attaq" phenomenon which had swept across the NBA and the nation's airwaves and marketplaces as well. Young and older fans alike collected and hoarded his memorabilia as they once had Jordan's and Magic's. A nation had fallen in love with his infectious personality. Those who never saw the Orlando Magic in even a single moment of televised NBA action nonetheless knew about the laconic giant who appeared in Pepsi commercials and pitched Reebok athletic shoes. Teenagers of all races now hummed his rap tunes or tapped out rhythms during his frequent MTV appearances.

And Shaq's rookie achievements, measured in simple basketball terms, were also impressive enough for any hardened skeptic. He was a landslide Rookie-of-the-Year selection and eighth-place finisher in the league MVP balloting as well. He was the only player ranked among the league's top ten in four different categories – eighth in scoring (23.4), second in rebounding (13.9), second in blocked shots (3.53), fourth in field-goal percentage (.562). He registered seven games with at least 20 points and 20 rebounds. He became the all-time Orlando team leader in blocked shots after a mere 34 games. And, last but not least, he joined a select circle of ten other active NBA players who have amassed 1,000 rebounds in a single season.

After only a single season in the big time Shaq O'Neal had miraculously become the nation's favorite athlete-superstar. He had also staked out his claim as one of basketball's best players with his "rookie-of-the-year" credentials and his strong-armed shot-blocking and slam-dunking play at both ends of the court. But he was still only just learning the game as it is now played at the highest levels of competition. Shaq was already poised to become perhaps one of the greatest NBA big men of all time. But it was clear, as well, that he had already declared the national media as his own personal playground. Shaquille O'Neal's coronation as the NBA's newest crown prince was now in full swing.

Left: *Orlando Magic number "32" is already almost as famous as the reverse digits "23" long worn by Michael "Air" Jordan. But the only name necessary to identify this superstar is sports' most universally recognized nickname – Shaq.*

Right: *A modern-day intimidator cut in the mold of defensive legends like Russell and Chamberlain, Shaq proves against Charlotte's Kenny Gattison that he can reject opposition slams with the same finality used in making his own.*

PART II
DON'T FAKE THE FUNK—SHAQUILLE O'NEAL TODAY

Shaq's most enthusiastic champions as well·as his most outspoken critics — and there are plenty of both — all seem to agree upon one thing without any reservation at all. It is Shaquille O'Neal the marketing marvel and TV pitchman, not Shaq the established basketball star, who has thus far enjoyed the greatest impact on his hordes of young and old fans alike.

Magic Johnson and Michael Jordan first captured the imagination of hoop fans a decade ago with their spectacular head-to-head performances during the NBA post-season. In the popular imagination of today's fan, however, Shaquille O'Neal breaks down backboards on promotional videos, not in regularly witnessed league action. In this sense the legend of the mythical basketball superhero has somewhat preceded that of the proven flesh-and-blood court star. As with so many of our current pop culture heroes, image has here outstripped actual performance.

"In Shaq," boasts Reebok company president Roberto Muller, "we already have the charisma of Magic Johnson, the talent of the NBA's legendary centers, and a personality that supersedes Michael Jordan." Muller points out, quite accurately, that it took Jordan about three years to reach the marketing impact that Shaq was already enjoying after only three months of circulation. And Reebok's executive spokesman is probably largely correct in his assessment of Shaq's charismatic edge over both Magic and Air Jordan. But when it comes to claiming that Shaq O'Neal already boasts the talent level of Wilt Chamberlain, Bill Russell, Kareem Abdul-Jabbar or Bill Walton — here the claims seem to be largely overstated.

There have been plenty of detractors to suggest that Shaq's pivot play needs a good deal of serious fine tuning before he can enter the pantheon reserved for the league's all-time greatest post-position players. Shaq

Left: *Shaquille O'Neal didn't take long to convince foes around the NBA that he was every bit what his press clippings claimed he was. In his first visit to the storied LA Forum in February 1993, the once-proud Lakers stood helpless as Shaq poured in 31 points and swept up 14 rebounds in a 110-97 Orlando victory.*

Right: *This crowd at the Bobigny Playground in Paris is evidence enough that Shaq is today an international celebrity whose fame spreads far beyond NBA arenas. Shaq visited France and numerous other European sites during a Reebok promotional tour in the summer of 1993.*

Left: *The power of Shaq's impact on rim and glass can almost be felt thanks to this unique camera angle from a backboard-mounted lens. Scott Skiles trails the play as O'Neal unleashes this famed Shaq-Attaq at Portland's Memorial Coliseum.*

Right: *Chicago's Scottie Pippen has nowhere to go as Shaq closes off the baseline in Chicago. Bullets coach Wes Unseld once asked if Shaq ever did anything besides dunk. Pippen discovers here that there is indeed more to O'Neal's game than slam shots.*

Below: *It's a king-sized shoe, and the familiar trademark makes it altogether clear which king it was meant for.*

may seem to demonstrate his worthiness to rank alongside Russell and Chamberlain and the others with a simple glass-smashing dunk during his widely aired Reebok commercial — the one in which Bill Russell asks for the magic password and the five great NBA centers sit in judgment on Shaq's thunderous dunk before admitting him into their select fraternity. In real life, however, these and other staid critics have been a bit more harsh in their judgment of Shaq's still rough-hewn on-court game.

Wilt, for one, sees little comparison at present between himself and Shaq the raw rookie. "I think this man is only going to get better and better," insists Wilt, "but he's going to have to be taught some inside offensive skills. He's already established that he's going to the basket, so the defense is always back on its heels. If he develops a little five-foot jumper, then he's going to be tremendous. I like Shaq's game a lot, but it seems to me that ninety per cent of his baskets are dunks, and ninety per cent of my baskets as a rookie were jump shots."

Of course, Wilt was the greatest finesse-style big man in the game's history. It was Wilt who revolutionized big-man play in the early 1960s by demonstrating with his array of fadeaway jumpers and finger-roll layups that a dominating center could be more than a towering slow-footed giant like the first great NBA

center, George Mikan. Wilt was a true giant who brought agility as well as raw size to the inside offensive game.

And Wilt also carved out his mark as the most fearsome rebounder basketball has ever known. As a Philadelphia Warriors sophomore in 1960-61 he averaged a still-unheard-of 27.2 rebounds per contest. This is two more for every single game of an entire season than Shaq's one-game high of 25, an Orlando Magic team record which Shaq set against the Washington Bullets. Wilt's career average of 22.9 rebounds, amassed across 14 seasons and more than a thousand games, is itself far more than most players today ever hope to collect in any single career-best game. Shaq might some day rebound with the ferocity of Wilt, but he will certainly never put up the same kind of numbers. Nor will he likely ever be the balanced offensive force that Wilt was.

Of course comparisons of Shaq's scoring and rebounding numbers with those of Wilt and Bill Russell are largely meaningless, as are all such hypothetical comparisons of stats from one sports age to another. Chamberlain and Russell still rank first and second in all-time NBA rebounding, but in their era shooting percentages around the league were much lower. This meant far more rebounds to be had by everyone. In today's highly evolved game there are far more unstoppable inside dunks, which translates into very few missed shots once the ball is taken toward the goal by a big man. One comparison of statistics for the 1960-61 season versus the 1993-94 NBA campaign reveals a drop in team rebounding average from 73 to 43. Again this translates into about 60 less available rebounds in every game that Shaq now plays as opposed to games from Wilt's era.

And if Wilt also scored like no one before or since — once averaging an astronomical 50-plus points for an entire 1961-62 league season — it was because of two factors that have also long since disappeared from the pro hoop scene. Philadelphia Warriors club owner Eddie Gottlieb encouraged Wilt's scoring binges. Racking up imposing offense numbers seemed the best way to promote the league in an age when fans came only in small handfuls. And Wilt played in a much shorter forest when he first appeared on the scene. There was but one rival 7-footer in the entire league the year Chamberlain entered the NBA, compared with 37 (along with 22 others measuring 6'11") strewn across last season's NBA lineup.

It is as a defensive intimidator — á la Bill Russell — where Shaq is most clearly cut in the mold of old-school NBA centers from years gone by. He is indeed something of a rare throwback to an earlier age of classic pivotmen whose game was pure bulk and brawn. The object of the classic power game is to anchor yourself near the middle of the lane, not far from the basket, then get the ball with your back to the basket and force the ball in as close to the hoop as possible. And at the defensive end of the court these hulks would simply close down any traffic entering a zone that stretched from the foul line to the hoop.

Wilt Chamberlain has been candid about the potential — as well as the flaws — he sees in Shaq O'Neal's emerging power-style game. Bill Russell has been

Far left: Another undervalued aspect of Shaq's developing game is his large presence without the ball at the offense end of the floor. Shaq here sets an effective screen for teammate Jeff Turner in Denver.

Below: Wilt Chamberlain (13) versus Bill Russell (6) was the titanic matchup of basketball's Golden Era in the 1960s. Fans today hope that Shaq will soon be playing Russell to David Robinson's Wilt the Stilt.

43

more reticent to comment on frequent comparisons between himself and Shaq and has carefully avoided statements regarding the newest pretender to a throne he once shared with Wilt alone.

Others, however, have been quick to compare these three great intimidators from different basketball eras. One such observer has been Wayne Embry, Russell's one-time understudy during the final years of the great 1960s-era Celtics teams, and now general manager of the Cleveland Cavaliers. "I see a lot of both Wilt and Russ in Shaq," concedes Embry. "Wilt was the strongest player of his day and that is where Shaq is right now. But Russell had that knack of moving laterally and shutting down the lane with his defense and shot blocking, and I see Shaq doing a lot of that as well."

O'Neal's major on-court weaknesses, then, are his largely one-dimensional offensive style and his under-developed passing and shooting skills away from the basket. No one questions the raw athleticism of his play, however. One observer cleverly noted that if Shaq does develop any new moves around the hoop it

Left: *Shaq may never have an unstoppable sky hook like the one Kareem Abdul-Jabbar patented. If Shaq did have such an effective outside shot to complement his powerful inside game, perhaps the entire rules structure of the game would need revamping to stop him.*

Right: *March 4, 1994 action between two classic centers of the 1990s: Shaquille O'Neal and Dikembe Mutombo of the Denver Nuggets.*

will be equivalent to King Kong barreling into some metropolis atop a tank. Shaq will certainly never be the versatile offensive package that Kareem Abdul-Jabbar once presented, with Kareem's unstoppable sky hook and unrivaled mobility around the bucket.

And so far he also remains a shade less effective near the basket than his main rivals for the title of today's premier big man – San Antonio's David Robinson, Houston's Hakeem Olajuwon, and perhaps even New York's Patrick Ewing. These three, unlike Shaq, all possess effective outside as well as inside games. They represent just as much instant offense when they step five or ten feet away from the bucket with their deadly jumpers as when they slam home unstoppable dunks. But the gap between Shaq and his more experienced rivals seems to be closing rapidly.

Perhaps the most meaningful and interesting comparison of NBA big men is between current heated rivals Shaq and David Robinson. Both are an identi-

cal 7'1″ in height, but "The Admiral" prefers to step outside, like a power forward, than rely on quickness to break free for a jumper or knife in for a sure layup. "I don't like to go 48 minutes of back-to-the-basket basketball," Robinson candidly admits. "Guys get a little nervous seeing me face-to-face against them."

So far Robinson has had the best of head-to-head competition with Shaq. O'Neal's only clear advantages against Robinson in face-to-face competition are the strength-intimidation factor and a slight ball-handling superiority. But in two meetings during Shaq's rookie campaign it was nowhere near enough. "The Admiral" thoroughly dominated the less versatile Shaq-Attaq, coming up with 23 points, 16 rebounds, seven assists, four steals and three blocks in their first-ever matchup, then returning with 30 points in their second encounter. After Shaq had led all league point-makers for most of 1993-94, Robinson also overhauled O'Neal down the stretch to capture the coveted scoring title. While both men averaged a shade under 30 points per game, it was Robinson and not Shaq who could boast of becoming the first pure post man to pace the league in scoring in several decades.

Robinson is one of several current league stars who has expressed occasional irritation at the seemingly constant hype surrounding the new glamor-boy of the NBA. Robinson has been terse in dismissing talk that O'Neal has already been crowned as the league's future big-man superstar. "He's pretty much got the same game as last year," Robinson recently observed, with obvious reference to his own domination over the inexperienced rookie.

NBA promoters and fans have to be thrilled with the

brewing rivalry, of course. NBA insiders are hoping that a Robinson-Shaq matchup will have all the flair that characterized the head-to-head combat of Philadelphia's Wilt Chamberlain and Boston's Bill Russell two decades ago.

NBA pundits also eagerly anticipate confrontation between Shaq and another dazzling 1993 rookie, Alonzo Mourning of the expansion Charlotte Hornets. Mourning enjoyed a great rookie campaign — averaging 21 points and 10.3 rebounds in 78 games — and would certainly have been the league's stellar rookie that year had it not been for the Shaq-man himself.

Head-to-head tussles between Mourning and O'Neal have thus far been slow to materialize, how-

Left: *Few veteran NBA observers would dispute that Houston's Hakeem Olajuwon is still the league's premier post player with his all-around talents and deadly shooting eye. Yet in one year Shaq has narrowed the gap enough that comparisons with Hakeem are no longer far-fetched.*

Right: *David Robinson battled O'Neal down the stretch of the 1993-94 season for the league's individual scoring championship. A 71-point game on the season's final day would allow San Antonio's "Admiral" (29.8 ppg) to edge Shaq (29.3 ppg) as the NBA's first center to pace the league since Jabbar 20 seasons earlier.*

ever. In the first scheduled face-off of headline rookies, Mourning was still riding the bench in the midst of an early-season contract dispute. When the schedule brought them together again late in the 1993 season, Shaq would display his own moment of poor judgment which ultimately cancelled another heralded meeting. With only slightly more than a dozen contests left and his Orlando team locked in a desperate struggle for the final divisional playoff slot, Shaq was uncharacteristically ejected and then suspended for a display of fisticuffs in the heat of an emotional contest with the rough-and-tumble Detroit Pistons. While a fine of more than $36,000 for a one-game suspension had small impact on Shaq's substantial wallet, the careless rookie had indeed hurt his team with his hot-headed moment of indiscretion. With Shaq on the bench Charlotte earned an easy victory and inched further ahead of Orlando in the tight playoff chase. And Shaq had also robbed fans of another chance to see the league's two brightest young stars lock horns.

The sophomore campaign for O'Neal and Mourning again largely meant postponement of their long-anticipated clash in the heat of NBA competition. Mourning spent most of the 1993-94 campaign on the disabled list and only returned for the season's final few

weeks. During the two encounters that did take place between the touted rookies in 1993, Shaq had a big statistical edge – averaging 29 points and 12.5 boards to 'Zo's 24 points and 11 rebounds. Still, Orlando and Charlotte seem destined to be one of the league's best future team rivalries, and Shaq versus 'Zo holds promise of all the drama provided by Shaq versus Robinson or Shaq versus Ewing. The NBA will soon boast not one titanic match-up recalling Wilt and Russell, but at least three. And all will feature Shaquille O'Neal front and center.

If Robinson and a handful of other NBA stars object to the glare of publicity cast on Shaquille O'Neal, this professional jealousy appeared to surge to the surface most notably during the 1994 NBA All-Star contest held at the Target Center in Minneapolis. It was to be Shaq's second straight All-Star Game start in as many years and the showcase game in which many observers expected O'Neal to step to the fore as basketball's new unchallenged headliner. But it didn't turn out quite that way.

Entering the All-Star weekend in Minneapolis Shaq was well on the way to disarming his early critics by leading the league in scoring while ranking second in blocked shots and among the top ten in rebounding. There was little doubt around the league that "Shaq

Left: *Shaq was double-teamed and tripled-team during the 1994 All-Star Game contest in the Minneapolis Target Center. The swarming and fouling defense meant a long afternoon for the still unpolished second-year player.*

Right: *While the press focuses on the headline matchups between Shaq and Robinson, Shaq and Ewing, or Shaq and Olajuwon, perhaps the true dream-match for years to come will be between O'Neal and multi-talented Alonzo Mourning of the Charlotte Hornets. "Zo" would have been a hands-down rookie-of-the-year choice in 1993 had Shaq not been around.*

Attaq II" was a fitting name for more than just O'Neal's latest line of Reebok footwear. The opposing All-Stars on the West squad – led by Robinson, Hakeem Olaju-won and Shawn Kemp across the front line – were determined, however, to put the towering youngster in his place, once and for all. And against a triple-teaming defense altogether unknown in previous All-Star classics, Shaq had a long afternoon indeed. Four of O'Neal's first five shoots were rejected; he made good on only two of twelve shots for the entire game. One thing the contest did once again underscore, of course, was Shaq's desperate need for a more flexible style of offense.

Commenting as a television analyst, Hall-of-Famer Julius Erving was one of the NBA experts who noted the lesson taught by the 1994 All-Star game shackling of the one-dimensional Shaq. "He simply has to learn to drop away from the bucket for the short jumper," Erving told the TV audience. "Only then will Shaq earn credentials as one of the all-time greats."

Shaq himself has been quick to react to such fla-grant "jealousies" among his NBA opponents. He was particularly stung by the tactics used against him during the All-Star matchup in Minneapolis, those attempts to "knock him silly" on every dunk attempt in what was, after all, merely an exhibition for the fans, with nothing in the form of prize money or league standings at stake. "It's because they can't do stuff I can do," contended an upset Shaq. "Jealousy is the ugliest word in the dictionary. I can do a whole

Left: *Shaq strikes an intimidating pose as Neon Bodeaux in the 1994 movie* Blue Chips.

Right: *Nick Nolte plays coach to Shaq's Neon Bodeaux at mythical Western University in* Blue Chips.

Below: *Shaq plays a role he knows well in* Blue Chips, *as Neon and teammates enjoy a championship celebration.*

bunch of things. Every time I do something, I do it well. My movie [*Blue Chips*] is doing well. My album [*Shaq Diesel*] will be platinum soon. So it's not like I'm good at one thing and sloppy at another. I'm just a man of many talents, and others don't understand that."

While Shaq might here be overlooking the professional pride of fellow All-Stars who felt motivated in Minneapolis to prove that they deserved a share of the media attention as well, it is in the end hard to argue with such frank assessment of his own personal success. If his on-court game could still be criticized for one-dimensionality, the same could hardly ever be

said about Shaq the multi-media performer.

While critics have been quick to find numerous flaws in the underdeveloped game of a celebrity rookie, Shaq himself has been busy in only his second NBA season making daily converts among many of his severest early detractors. Despite a truly dizzying schedule of off-season promotions during the summer following his rookie campaign, somehow the tireless O'Neal found a way to upgrade his low-post game almost nightly. A month or two into his sophomore season he was already silencing some of the biggest naysayers. And by late season he had already come close to living up to much of the hype surrounding

Left: "I think you have to go back to Wilt Chamberlain to find somebody as big and strong as Shaquille. But whenever we played against Wilt, we always had somebody who could match him. We don't have that right now when we play Shaquille." – Coach Wes Unseld, Washington Bullets. And it seems as though no other team has anyone to match up with Shaq either.

Right: The NBA clearly misses the magical appeal of Michael Jordan (seen here with Clyde Drexler), with his trademark extended tongue and flashy playing style. The marketing of Shaquille O'Neal has now become a crucial part of the league's efforts to minimize the loss of its most popular player ever.

Shaq the basketball phenom.

For one thing, Shaq's offensive numbers throughout much of his second season indicated a vastly improved total offensive game. For much of the season he paced the league in scoring, hovering a fraction under the 30 points-per-game mark. This was nearly a six-point increase over his respectable rookie average which had placed him only eighth among NBA point-makers. Shaq's rebounds were down ever so slightly to 13 per game from his rookie 13.9 average. Yet he again stood second only to Dennis Rodman in this important category. Shaq's field goal percentage had jumped from a rookie fourth-best .562 to a second-place .602 standard. The faceoffs with rival star centers were beginning to swing more Shaq's way, however. And the result was a legitimate charge toward a playoff spot for the Orlando Magic, who owned the fourth best Eastern Conference won-lost record entering the season's final long month.

One of the best examples of Shaq's improvement came in a late March 1994 game against the powerhouse New York Knicks, owners of the best Eastern Conference record. The contest was billed as another test-match between Shaq's inside power game and Patrick Ewing's refined finesse-style post play. The Knicks would dominate the nationally televised prime time contest, 111-90, and Ewing would enjoy a fine outing with a game-best 31 points and 11 boards. But Shaq again more than held his own against his more polished rival, tallying 30 points of his own and winning the rebound contest with 16. No longer could Ewing dominate the Shaq-Attaq as he had in their final meeting of Shaq's rookie tour.

Former pivot star Bill Walton — another basketball "free spirit" who did things his own way — is one of those quick to see the improvement during Shaq's second NBA season and to dismiss criticism of Shaq's

apparent lack of off-season concentration on basketball. "Simply look at his stats," notes the Hall-of-Famer. "He's leading the league in scoring, is second in blocked shots and among the leaders in rebounding. Those are some pretty good numbers and they tell me he must have been doing something right with his game over the past summer."

A second well-respected voice to comment positively on the vast improvements in Shaq's overall game is big-man guru and Hall-of-Fame former coach Pete Newell. Newell has built a wide basketball reputation over the past several decades for his outstanding work in molding the game's top post players. And if some NBA purists are offended by O'Neal's sudden celebrity and by the chinks in his basketball armor, Newell is not among them. The legendary coach is lavish in his praise for the work ethic Shaq has brought to his steadily improving game.

"Listen, that's a most ridiculous thing to say, that he doesn't work at his game," Newell observes about Shaq. "He just does a lot of things and is one of those people who is a doer. He's got a real good work ethic, and he's just about as pliable and easy to teach and receptive as anybody I've ever had." This coming from a veteran tutor who has worked over the years with just about every one of the game's up-and-coming seven-footers.

Newell sees Shaq as a pretty "all-together guy" and a star pupil in basketball technique. "You know what the kid has? He has wisdom. He's got a maturity about him, and the more you get to know him the more you realize this." And Pete Newell should know as much as anyone. Newell, after all, has put in plenty of time with Shaq, both at Newell's renowned Big Man Camp, and also as special adviser for Shaq's role in the film *Blue Chips*.

Newell also sees the current bashing of Shaquille O'Neal as being something akin to the earlier put-downs that surrounded the career of Michael Jordan. "First Jordan couldn't shoot outside, according to his critics," Newell observes. The way Newell views it, as soon as Jordan developed his game to the point where he would can three-pointers with regularity his critics just as quickly rallied around another supposed flaw in his game. "He has the ball too much" was one complaint; "He's not enough of a team player" was another.

With Shaq, Newell sees the same kind of irrational badmouthing. "People say that all he does is dunk, but that's a lot of crap. I mean, he's got spin moves, he's got step-back moves, he's got a little hook. But when a guy can explode the way he can explode, why shouldn't he exploit that?"

A majority of fans seem to have little difficulty with the predictability of Shaq's one-way power approach to playing basketball. When the final two roster spots were named in March 1994 for a "Dream Team II" All-Star squad that would represent the United States in the World Cup that summer, Shaquille O'Neal was an obvious choice for selection. More telling still, however, were the results of a *USA Today* readers' poll designed to tab fans' preferences for Dream Team honors. Shaq was a runaway popular choice, polling 32 per cent among votes tallied. Rookie Chris Webber of the Golden State Warriors finished a distant second with barely half of Shaq's winning total.

And for teenage fans who elect Shaq as their idol of choice there needs to be little convincing of the type that a basketball guru like Pete Newell would offer. Shaq's younger and more impressionable fans are swayed by image and not by subtle points of the fine-tuned NBA game. And when it comes to image there is no questioning who rates "number one" with fans among today's NBA superstars.

The Shaq portrayed in TV commercials is a colossal and intimidating yet lovable giant. He thus fulfills both the teenager's fantasy of incredible unstoppable power and the parentally sanctioned image of a more gentle sort of humanity. It is admittedly a carefully crafted made-for-marketing image, but a most effective one indeed.

In one popular commercial promoting Pepsi Cola, Shaq is seen entering a schoolyard playground occupied by young children. Shaq towers above the youngsters as he bends forward a basketball hoop and drops a ball through the lowered rim. But the awesome Shaq is held at bay by a spunky little boy who clutches a single remaining full bottle of Pepsi and rebuffs the giant's request for a drink. "Don't even think about it!" the brash youngster tells the chagrined giant of a superstar. Shaq bows his head as if beaten – the perfect gentle giant image.

The most recognized and widely distributed Shaq commercial, to be sure, is the one that candidly and even humorously addresses his current status in the pro basketball world. Here a bold Shaq knocks at the gateway entrance into basketball immortality. The gatekeeper – a gray and aging Bill Russell – demands a password while other Hall-of-Fame centers from the game's past – Bill Walton, Kareem Abdul-Jabbar, and Wilt Chamberlain – passively watch. With the boldness and hipness of the 1990s, Shaq answers his judges: "Don't fake the funk on a nasty dunk!" Shaq then demonstrates his "qualifications" with a backboard-shattering dunk of his own design. In the final scene, Shaq is ordered to pick up the shattered glass before entering.

Shaq's password response in the famed Reebok ad is clearly a reminder of his fondness for rap music. And when a self-satisfied Shaq stands before his judges with shattered rim and backboard proudly in hand, only to be given a broom and tray and told to clean up the mess, he responds with a subdued puzzlement: "It must be some rookie thing." Here once again was a perfect play on the unselfconsciousness of the towering youngster's rare sense of humor.

The real debate surrounding Shaq's celebrity status, of course, ultimately focuses on something other than his readiness to wear the mantle as one of the game's greatest-ever big men. Few serious basketball followers would truly expect that any rookie or sophomore should be judged so early by such impossible standards. What seems more troubling to Shaq's detractors is the issue of whether or not he can

Left: *Popular with fans of all ages, Shaquille O'Neal autographs basketballs for the faithful.*

Right: *Shaq seems as comfortable and confident performing a rap tune as he is splitting the nets or sweeping the boards in front of NBA game-action cameras. Here he raps for a French audience at the Zenith in Paris with his favorite rap group, Fu Schnickens.*

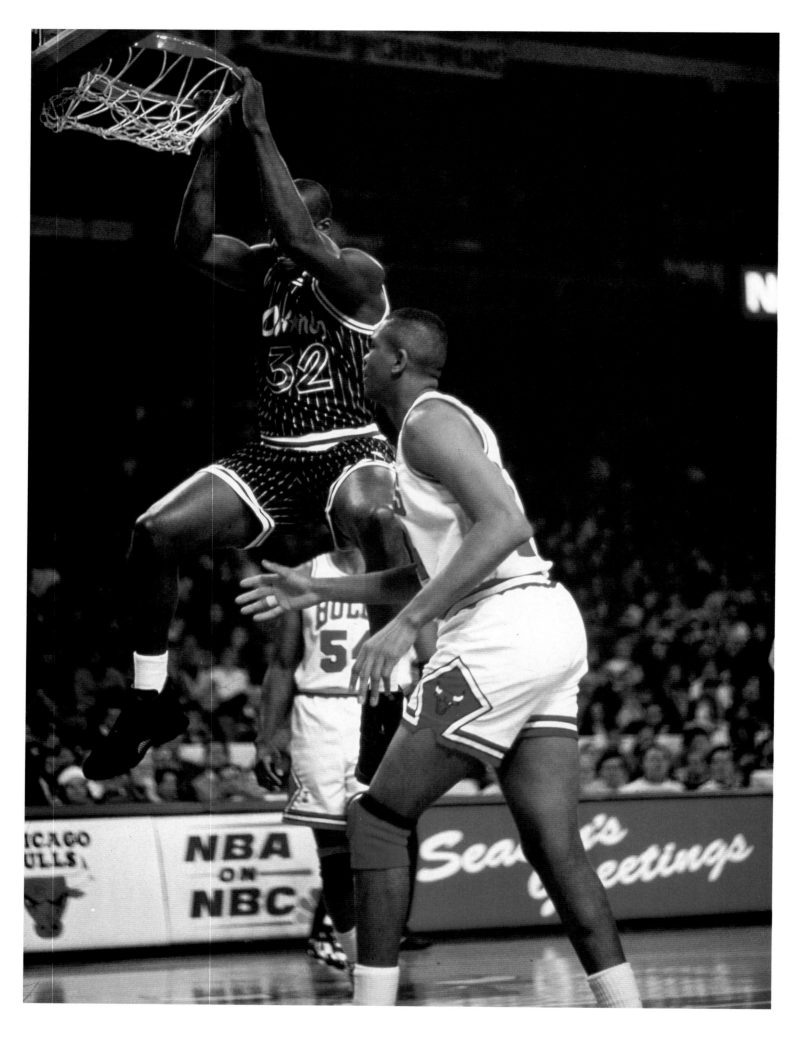

Right: *As a mega-celebrity instantly recognized anywhere he travels, Shaq needs the companionship of special security forces to keep the crush of his fans in check.*

Left: *The Shaq-Attaq is here unleashed in Chicago Stadium and splits a Bulls defense comprised of Horace Grant (54) and Bill Cartwright. "To see a 7-foot guy run like he does, jump like he does, and have the strength he has, is just unfathomable to most people," observes the Spurs' David Robinson.*

possibly be taking basketball — and thus his role as an NBA up-and-comer — all that seriously. After all, shouldn't he have been working more arduously on his flawed game during the summer months following his rookie season? Shouldn't basketball as his chosen profession be taking precedence over movie roles and worldwide marketing tours for consumer products?

Shaq himself certainly doesn't see it that way. For Shaq there are no given limits on how much his youthful energy can accomplish. "I'm young and I don't get tired," is the way Shaq rebuffs his doubters. "When people present you with all the opportunities

I've had, it's pretty tough to turn them down. But I also think I've been able to keep it in perspective. I understand that my real job is still basketball and that everything else is merely secondary."

Officials of the Orlando Magic seem equally undisturbed by Shaq's whirlwind off-court life. Pat Williams, the Magic's general manager, agrees that a Shaq bonanza is also an NBA bonanza and an Orlando bonanza as well. "We got more than we ever dreamed of in Shaq. His impact on basketball, in this country and around the world, went far beyond anything we could have predicted."

For Shaq himself it has been a bonanza that he

must now accept as something of a mixed blessing. His record $40 million NBA rookie contract is now already overshadowed by endorsement deals worth more than $50 million. Those deals have resulted directly from a brilliant marketing strategy designed from the outset by Shaq's talented agent, Leonard Armato. But these deals have also meant a huge burden of extra work and endless travel. Shaq's fame and wealth have not come without a stiff price of their own.

Whatever basketball purists may think of Shaq's hectic off-court life, it is certainly true that no profes-

sional basketball player — not even Michael Jordan — has ever been quite so much in demand away from the NBA arenas. Shaq's 1993 summer itinerary itself demanded almost superhuman strength to complete. Perhaps only a highly conditioned athlete with Shaq's indomitable spirit could have completed such a rigorous agenda.

First came a whirlwind Reebok tour of the Far East during which Shaq sandwiched press conferences and handshakes with company executives between endless slamdunking demonstrations for crowds of photographers. The tour was launched with a visit to

Japan during which the NBA's brightest star compared notes with headliners of Japan's sporting world, champion sumo wrestlers. A life-size fold-out Shaq poster promoted the visit in one Japanese magazine and a special Shaq commercial aired, complete with rap soundtrack that needed no translation.

This was followed by another Reebok junket, this time throughout Europe. The ubiquitous O'Neal put in an action-stopping appearance at the company's sponsored three-on-three basketball tournament in the Italian city of Milan. He greased palms and demonstrated a few "inside moves" for hordes of fans and press corps in Paris and Madrid as well. It was indeed true, as Reebok's president had earlier contended, that the company has gotten even more than they could have possibly anticipated from their windfall contract with basketball's first post-Michael Jordan megastar.

Ultimately Shaq's luminous star will rise still further, or it will eventually crash and burn, largely on the basis of his ability to prove himself as Air Jordan's anointed heir — the new basketball superhero. If Shaq's game continues to improve as it has in only a single season — if he leads his team to championships or crams his personal trophy case with rows of individual scoring and rebounding titles — then past stars like Russell, Chamberlain and Abdul-Jabbar may indeed have to make way for the sport's new super-charged big man. Certainly no previous NBA "big man" has ever been more charismatic from the very outset. And none — not even Russell in his prime — has had more dramatic impact on America's favorite sport of basketball, than has the Shaq-Attaq: Shaquille O'Neal.

Left: Shaq is developing a jump shot to go with his arsenal of power inside moves, a fact which has to be bad news for opponents everywhere around the NBA.

Right: The omnipresent Shaq takes a rare moment of rest on the Orlando bench.

INDEX

PHOTO CREDITS